BUGS

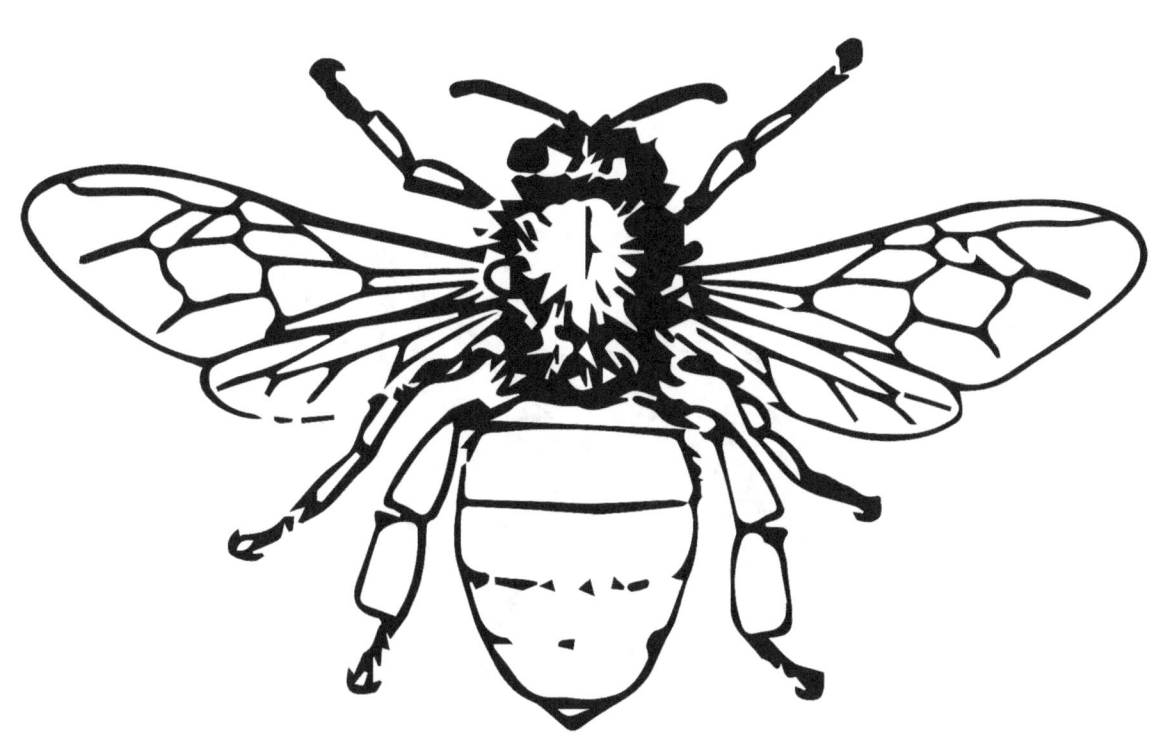

INSECT COLORING BOOK

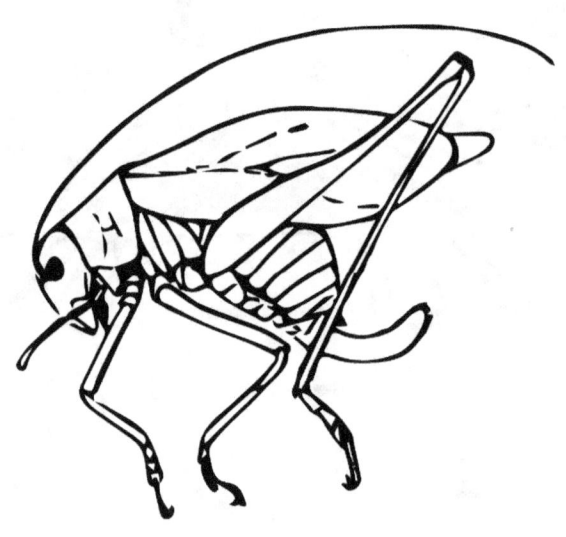

ISBN-13: 978-1533534637
ISBN-10: 1533534632

USE THESE PAGES TO TEST COLORS FOR YOUR BUGS

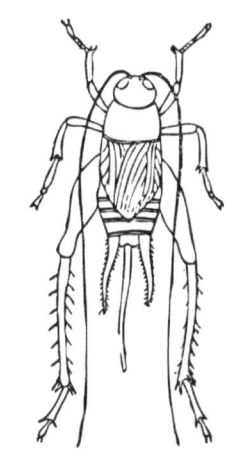

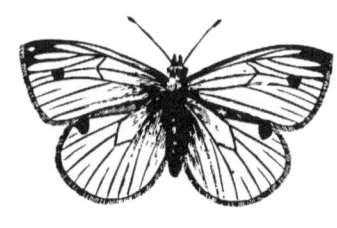

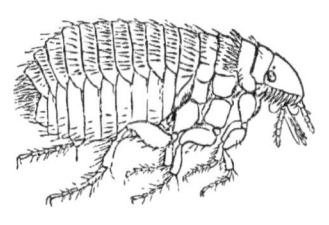

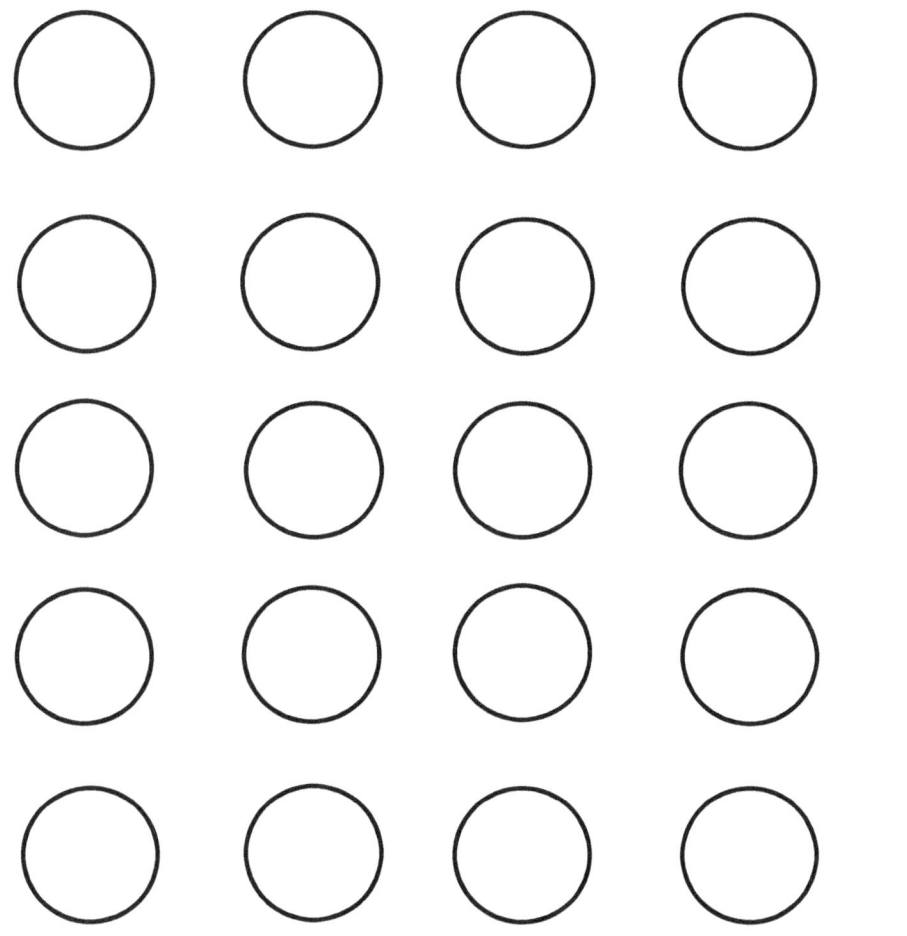

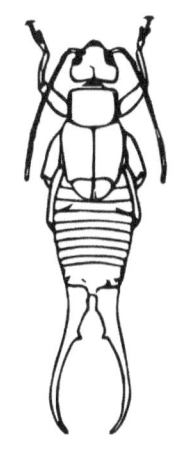

USE THESE PAGES TO TEST COLORS FOR YOUR BUGS

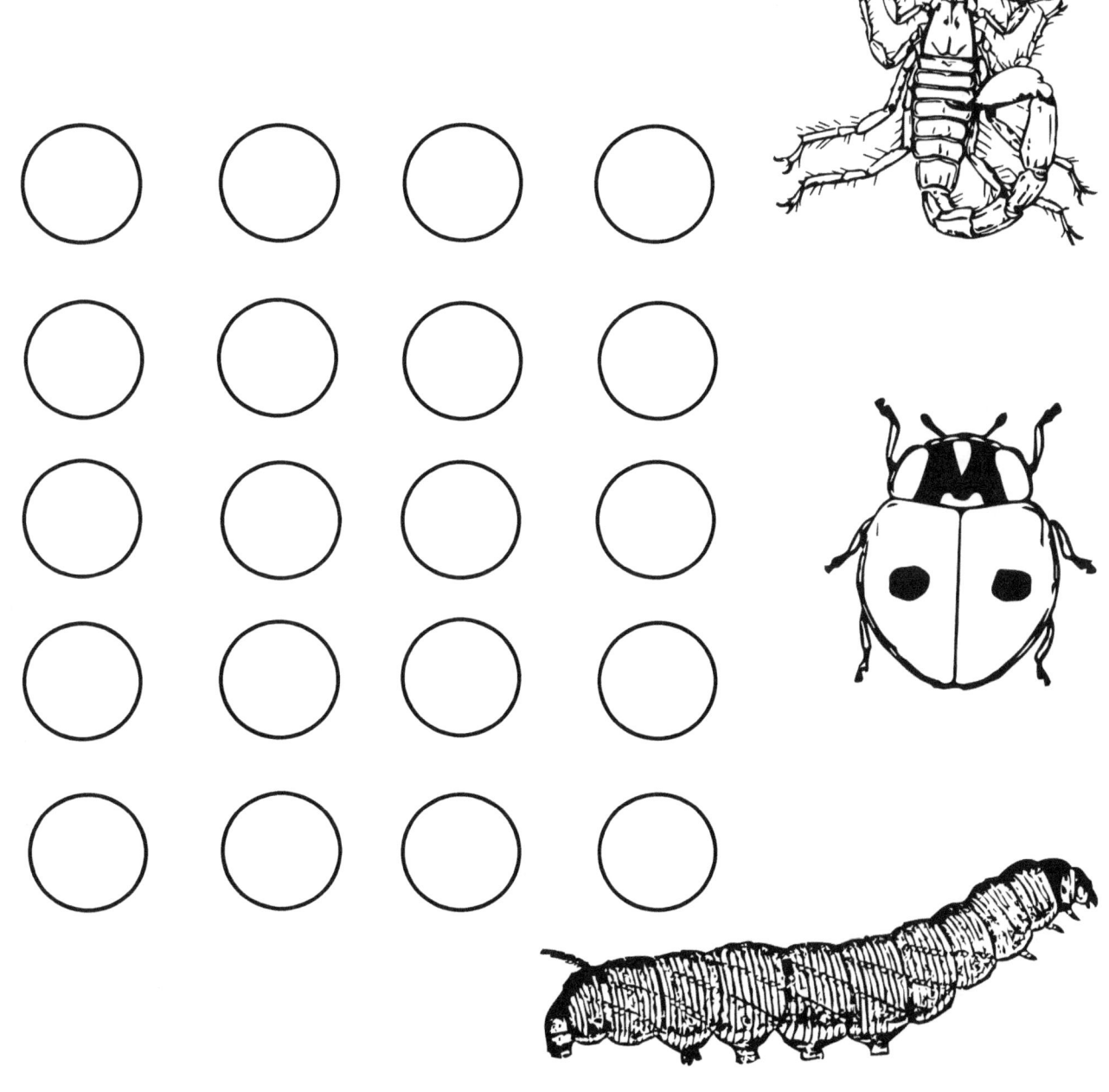

PLEASE NOTE:
TO ALLOW FOR LARGER
COLORING AREA, SOME BUGS ARE
PLACED TO TAKE ADVANTAGE OF
VERTICAL PAGE HEIGHT.

HAPPY COLORING!

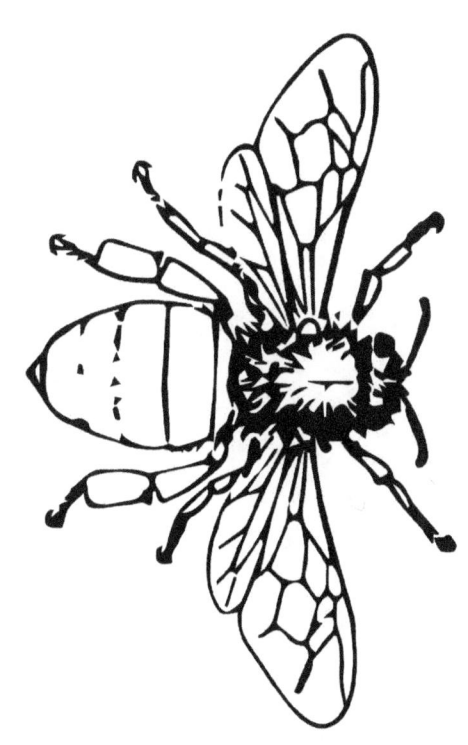

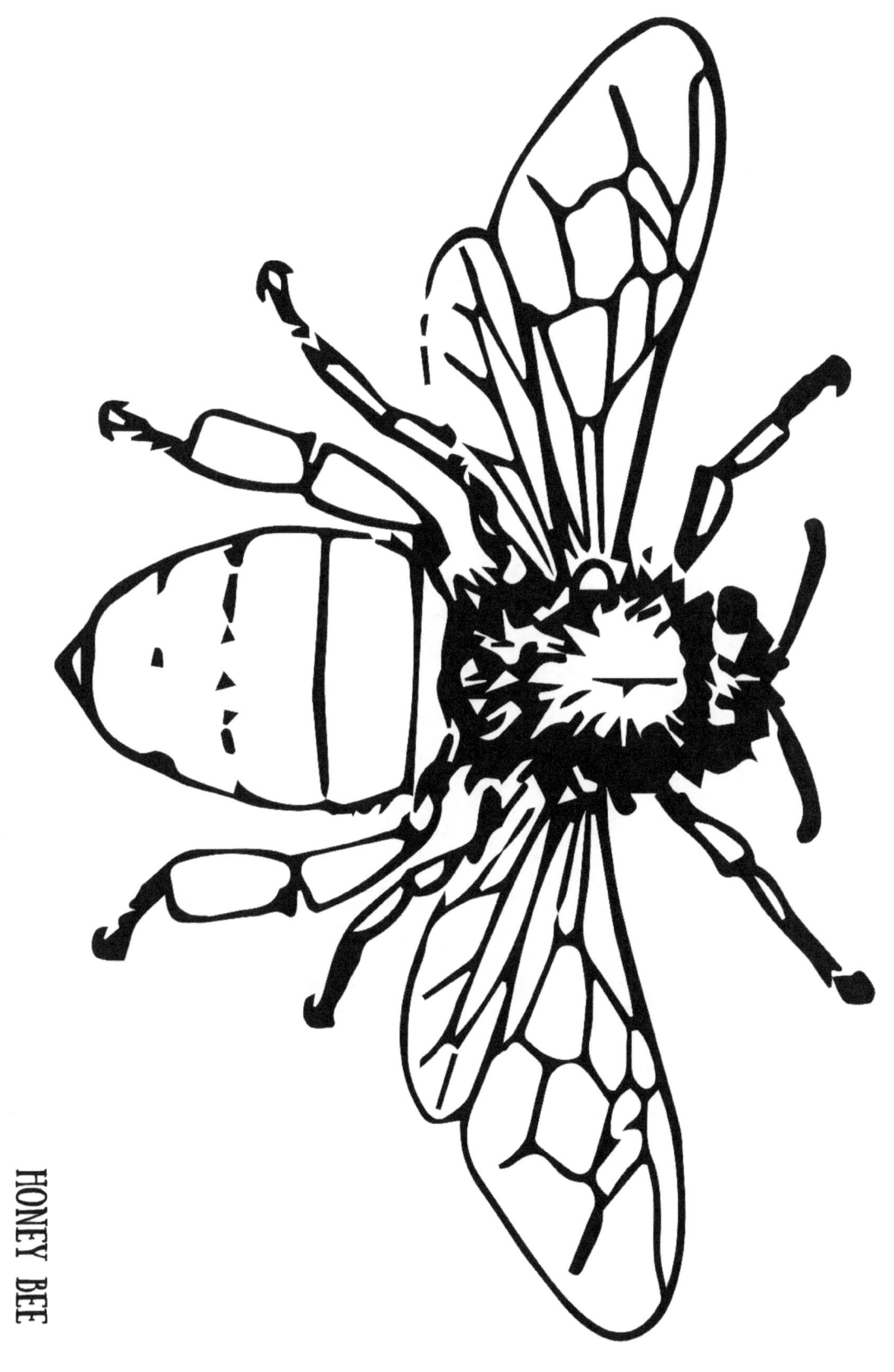

HONEY BEE

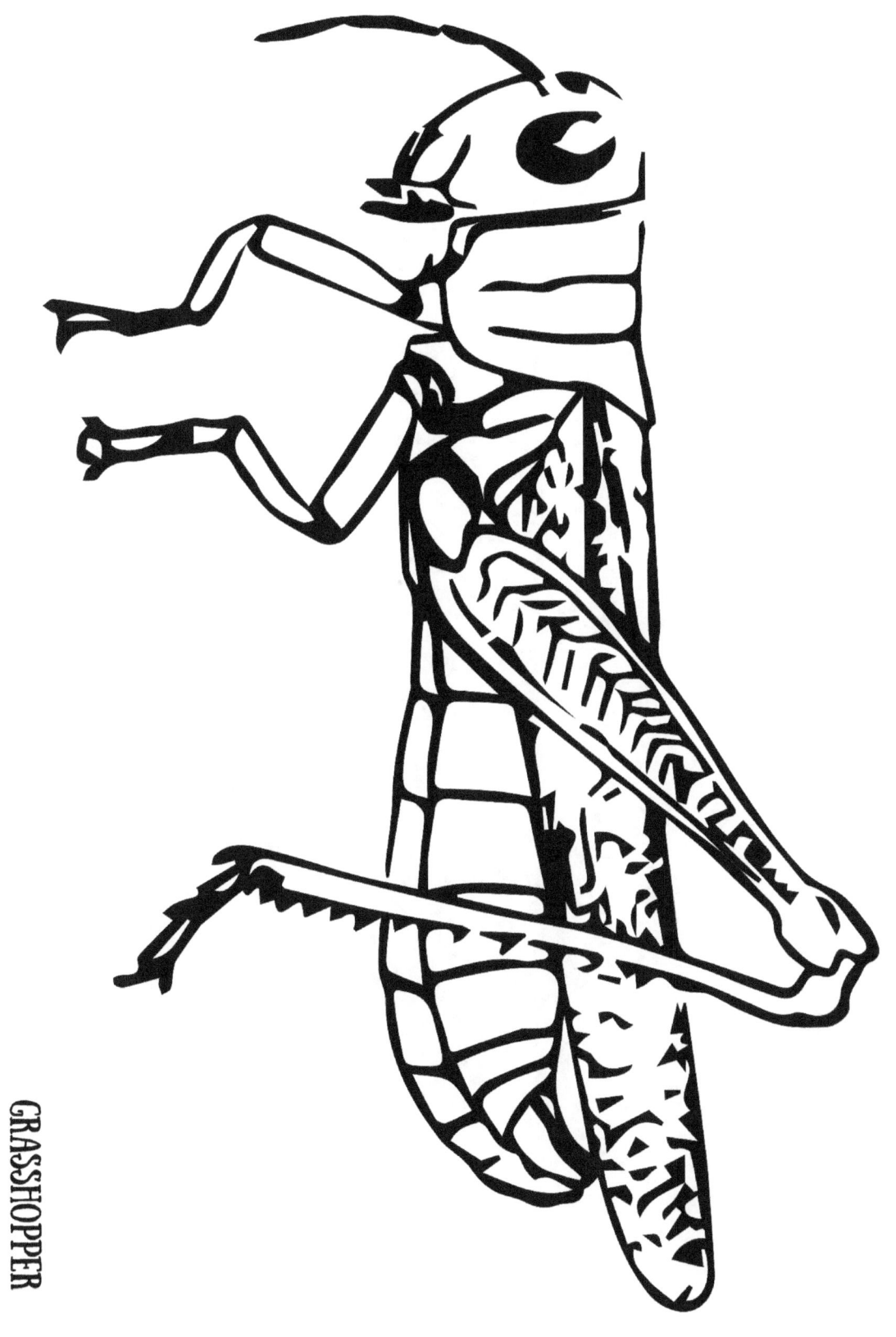

GRASSHOPPER

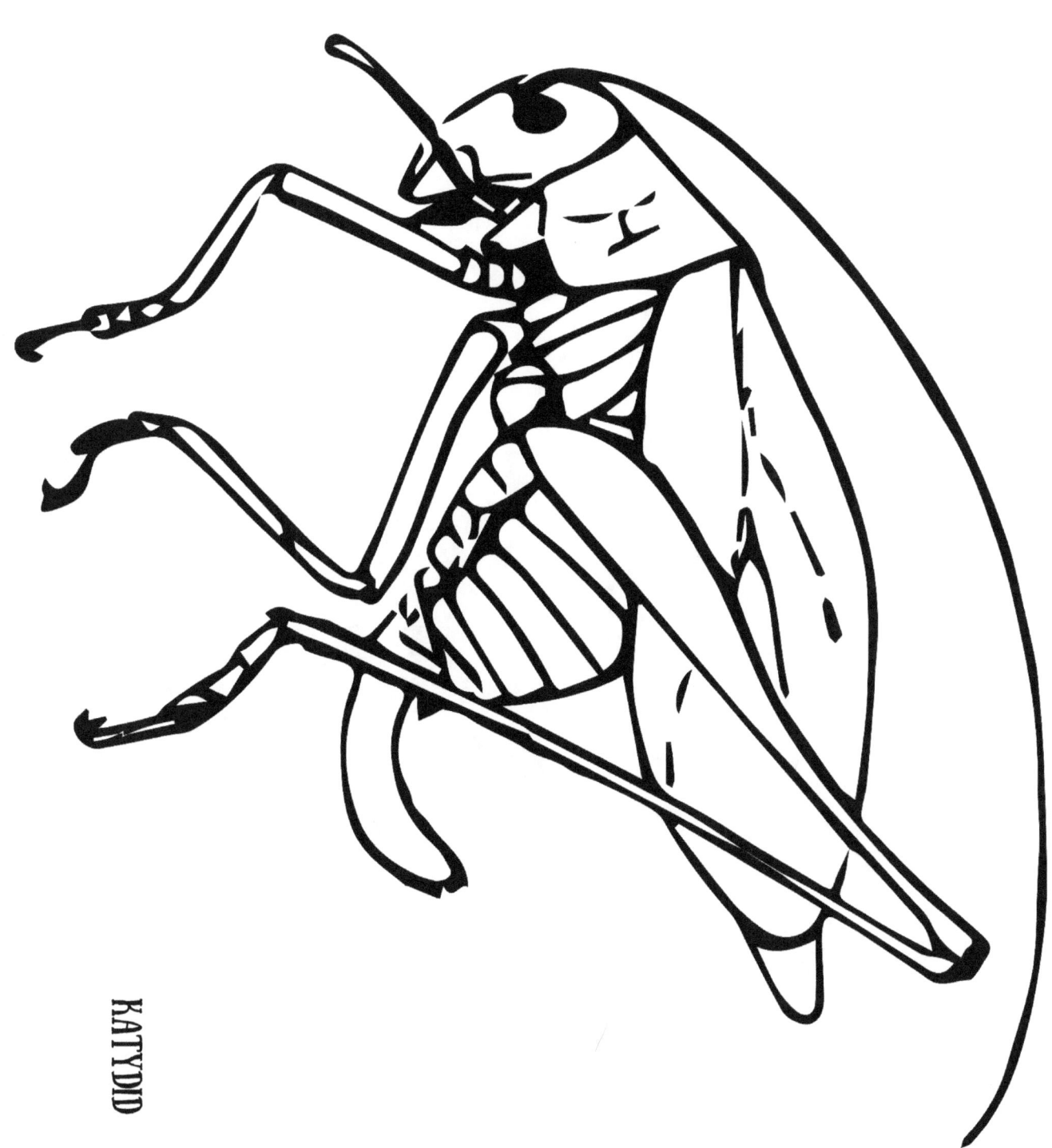

KATYDID

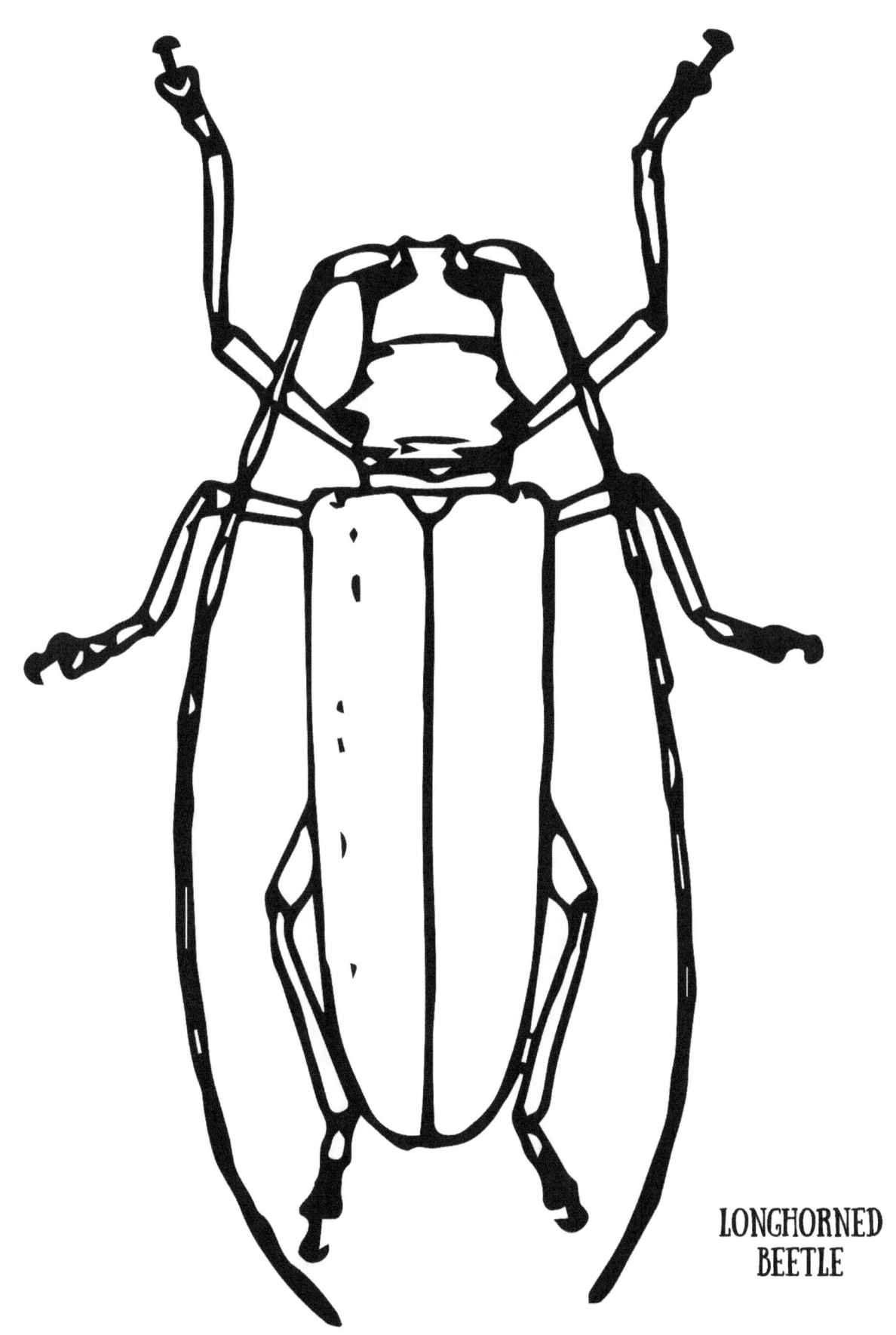

LONGHORNED
BEETLE

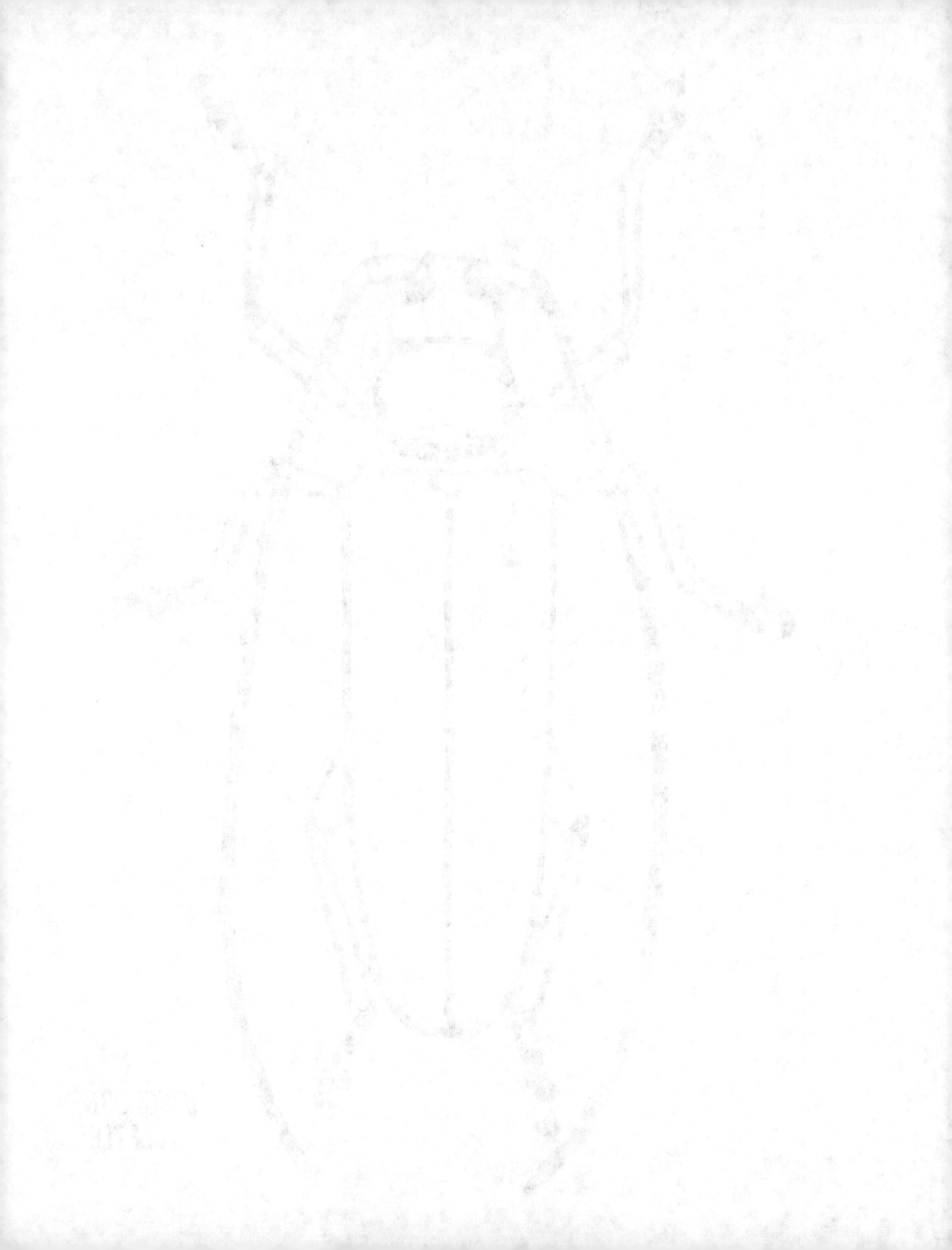

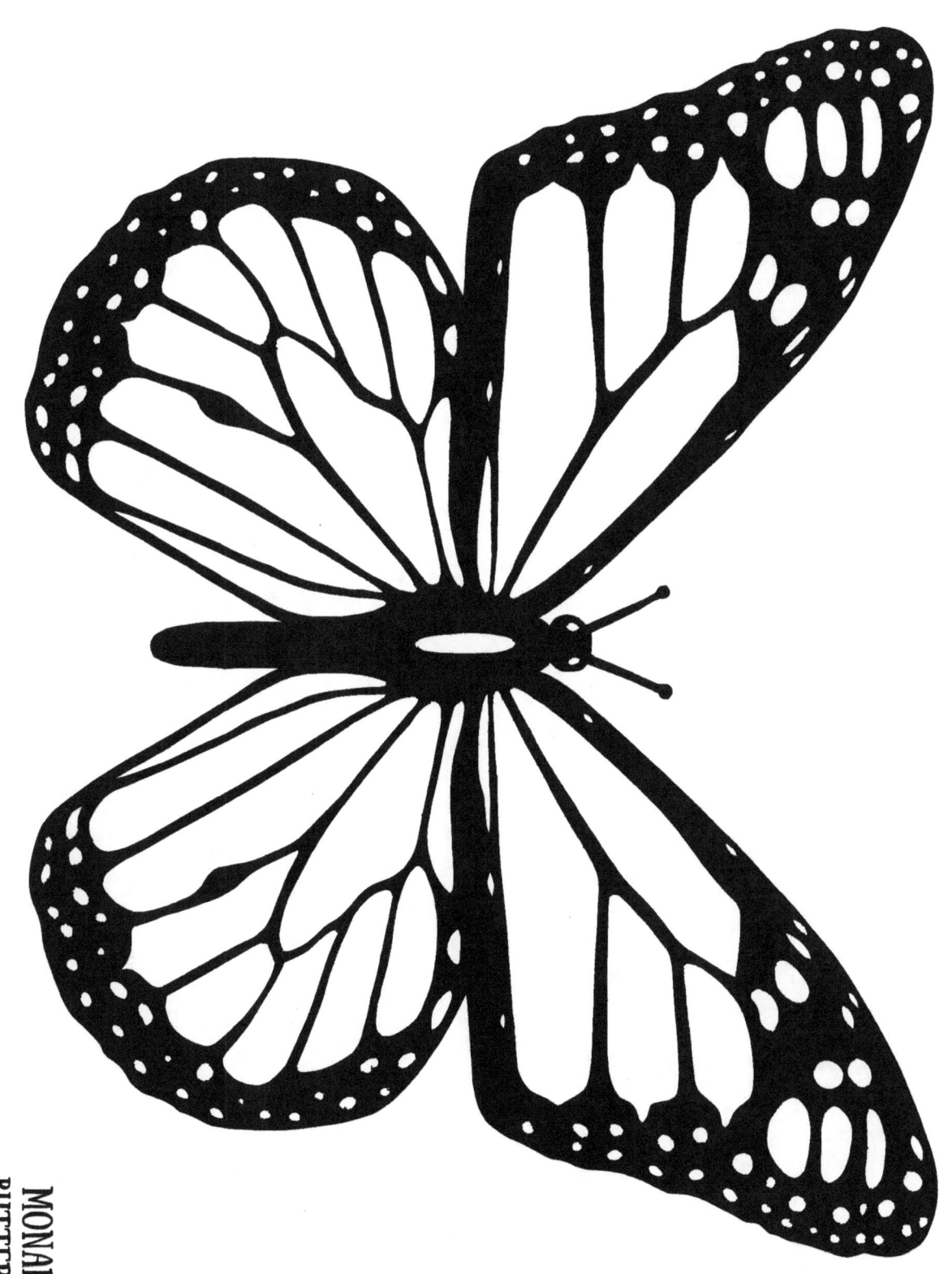

MONARCH
BUTTERFLY

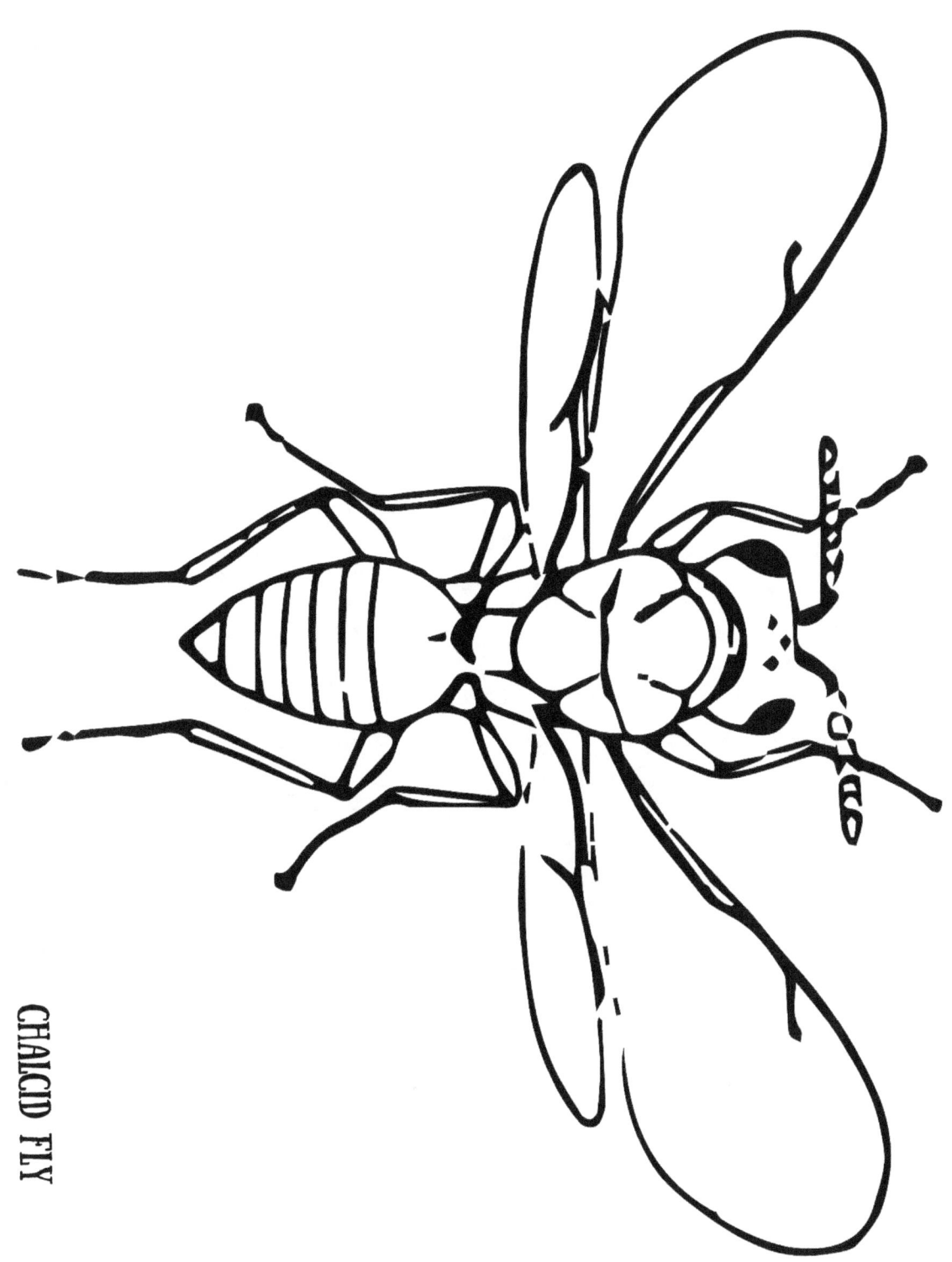

CHALCID FLY

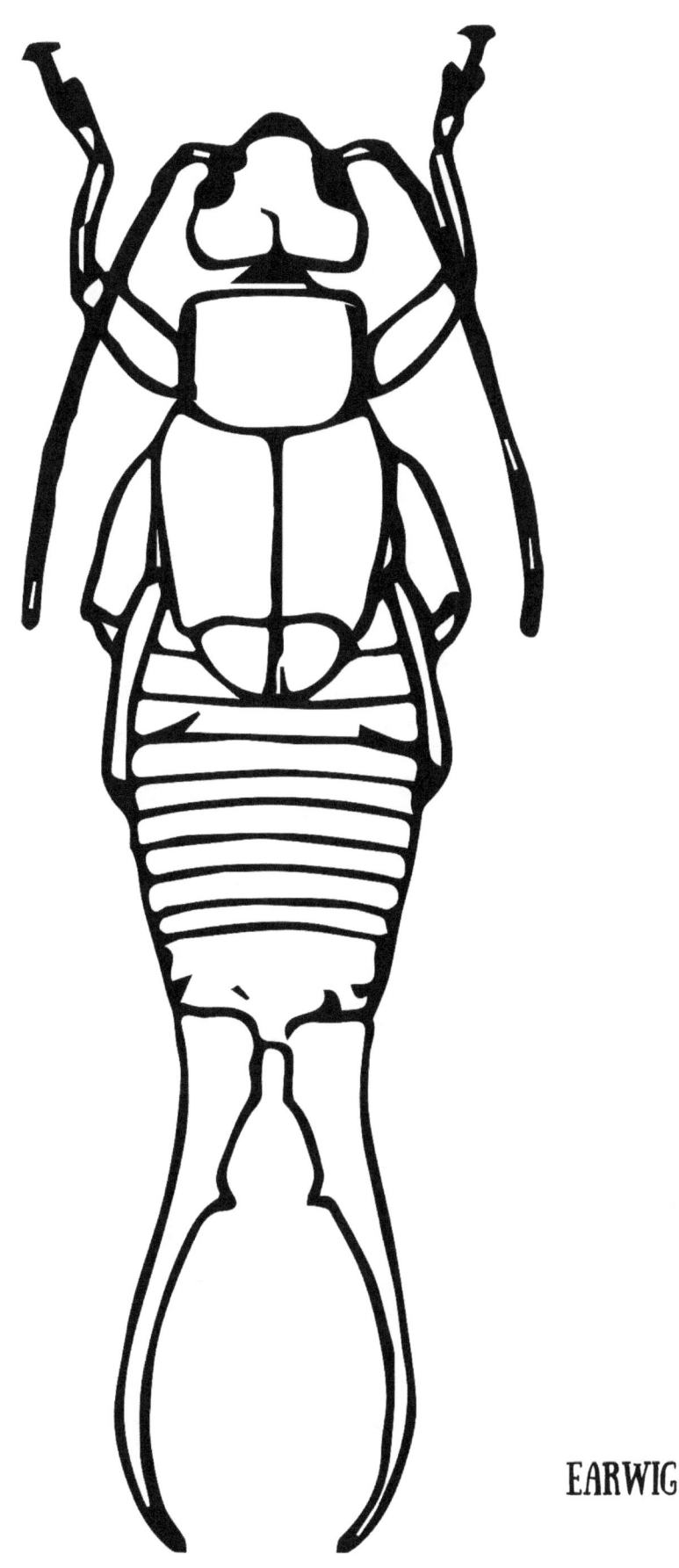

EARWIG

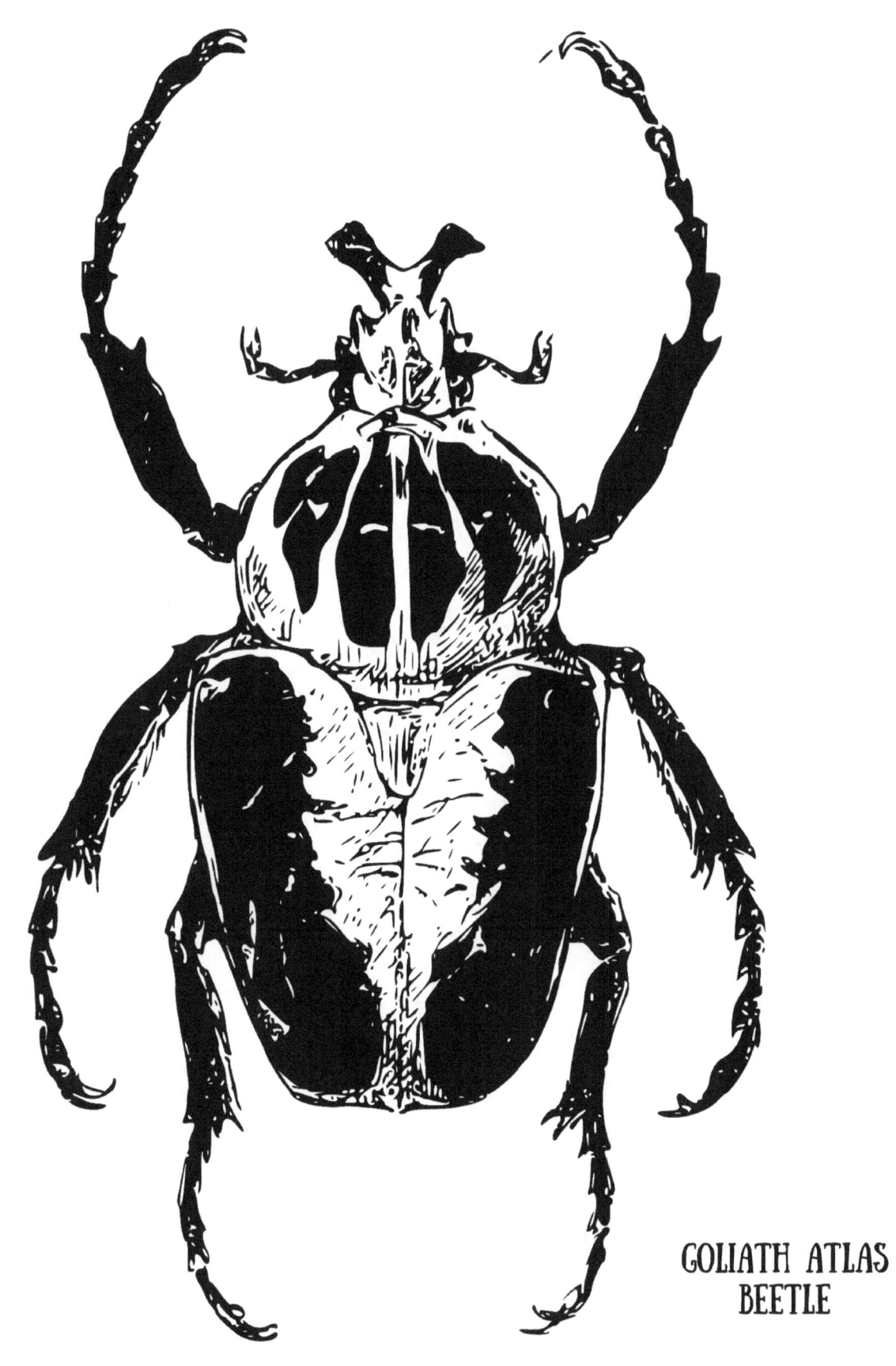

GOLIATH ATLAS
BEETLE

ICHNEUMON FLY

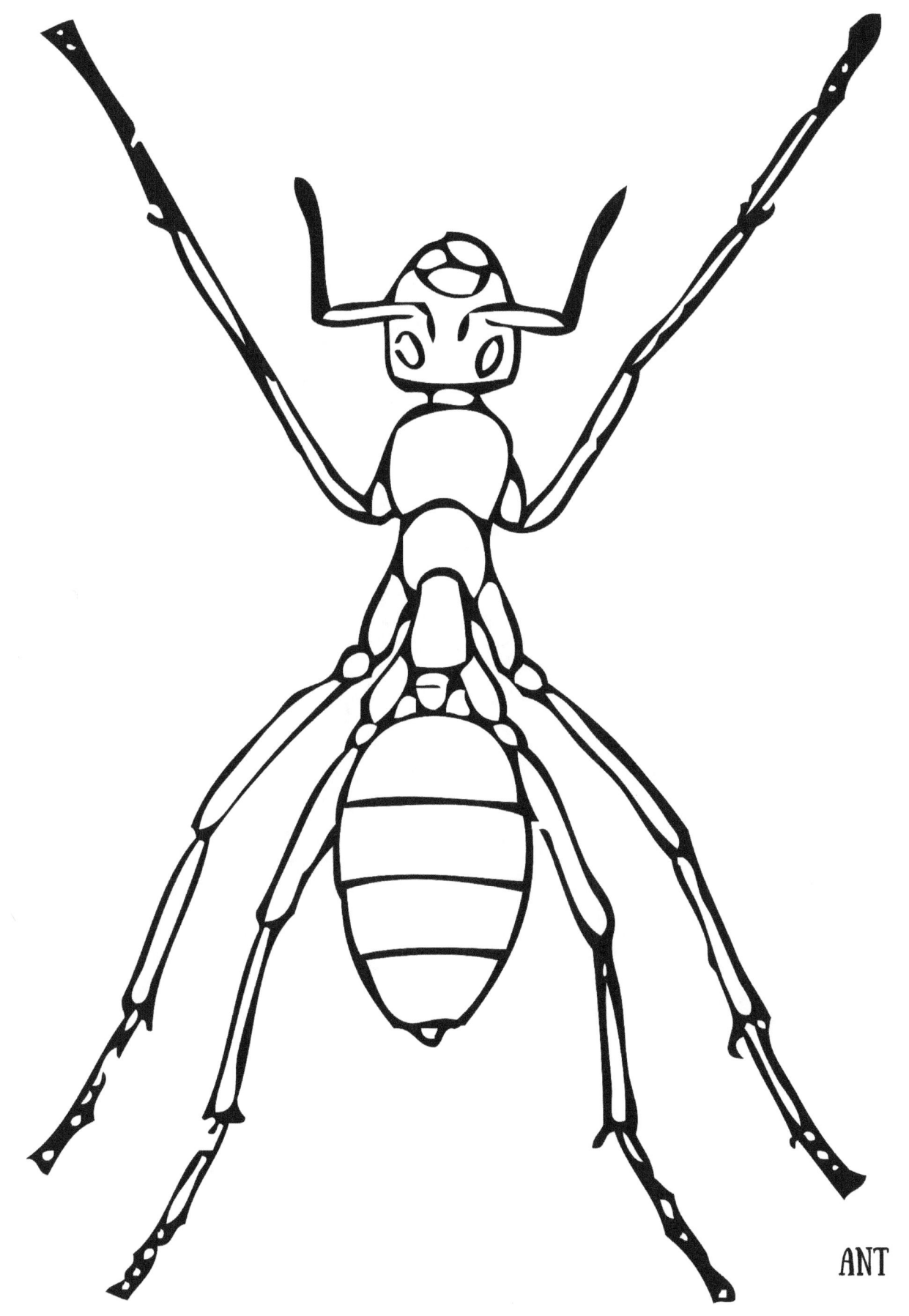

ANT

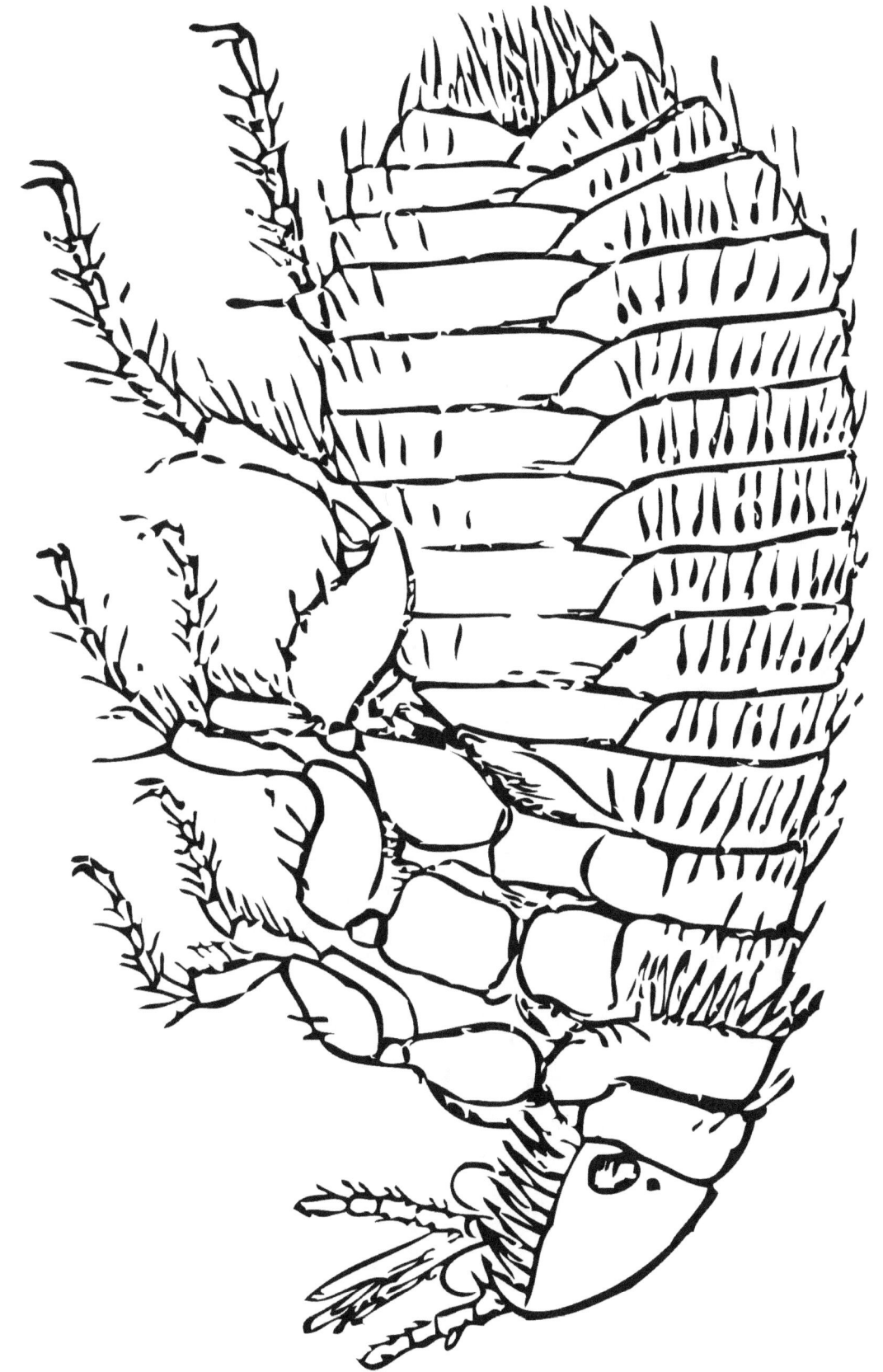

FLEA

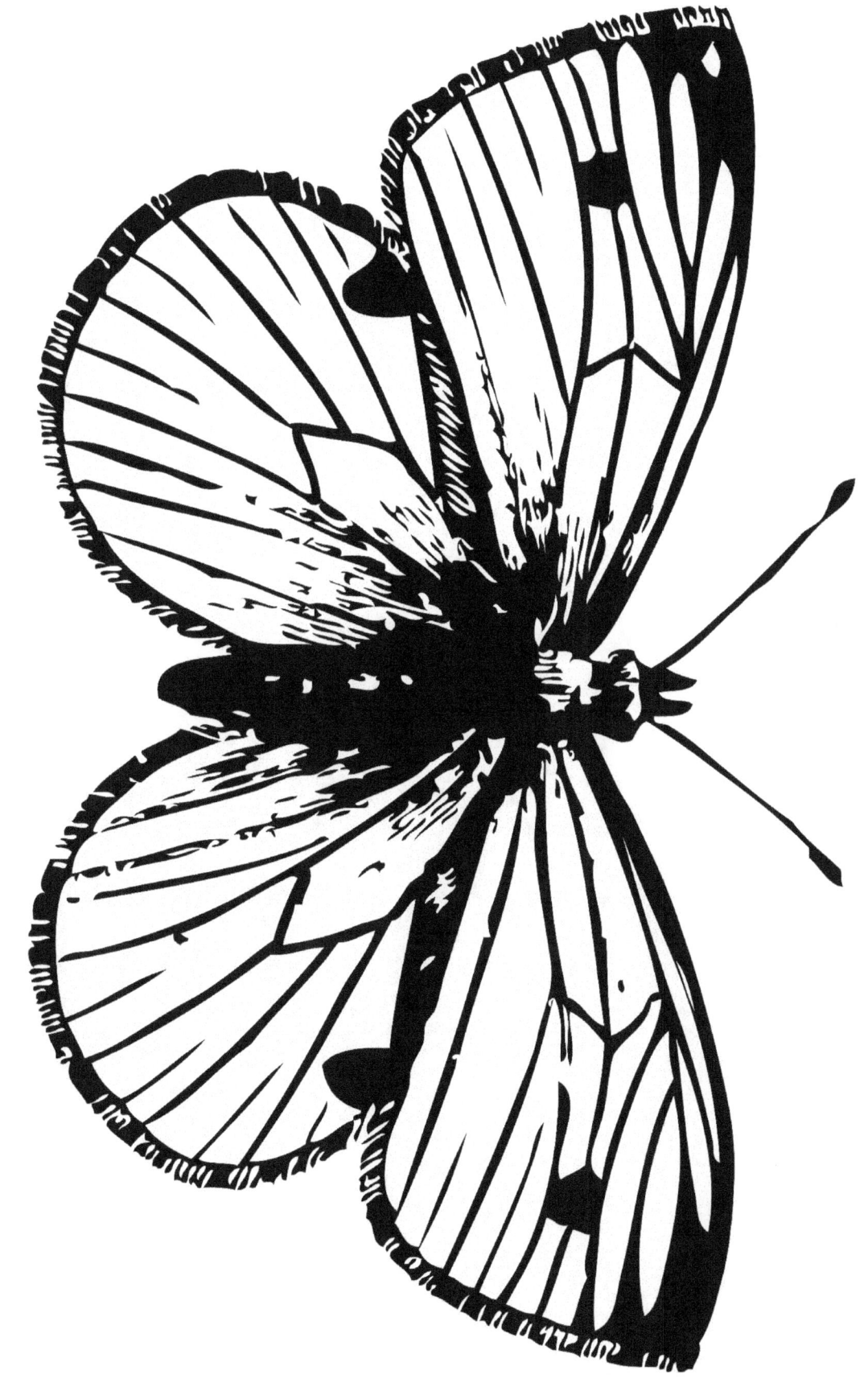

CABBAGE MOTH

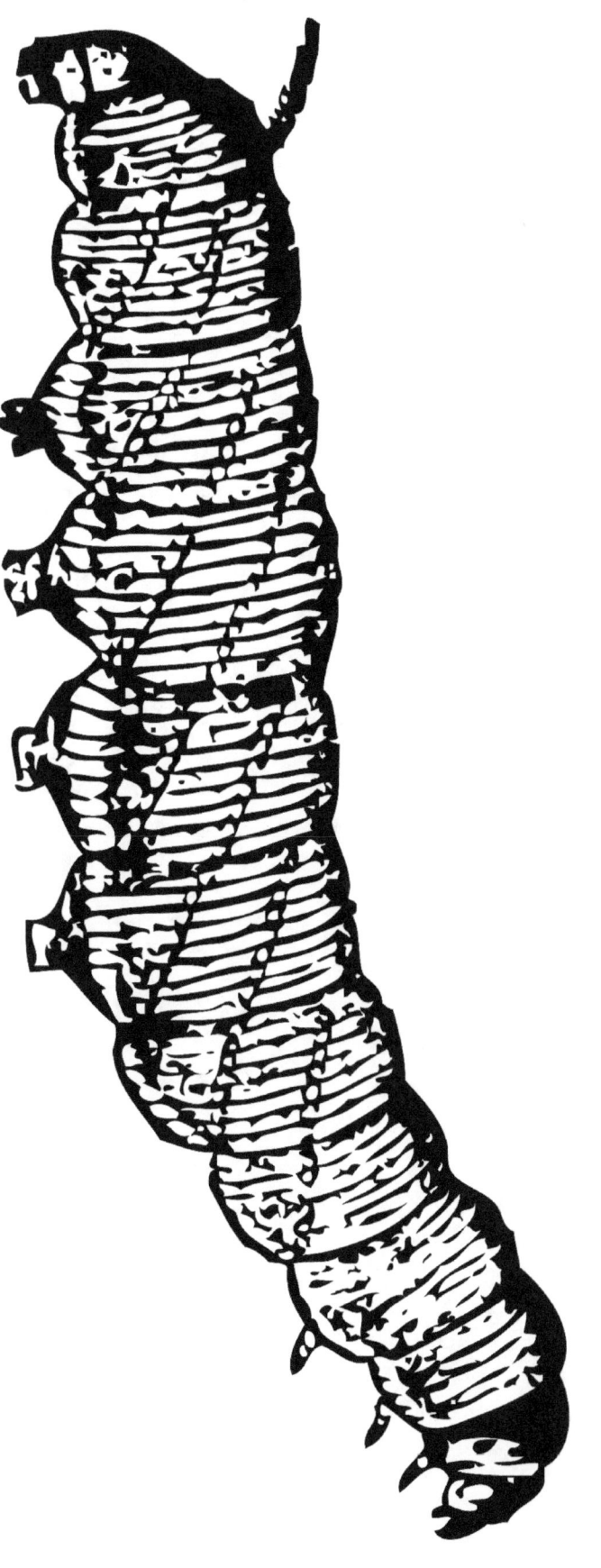

CATEREPILLAR

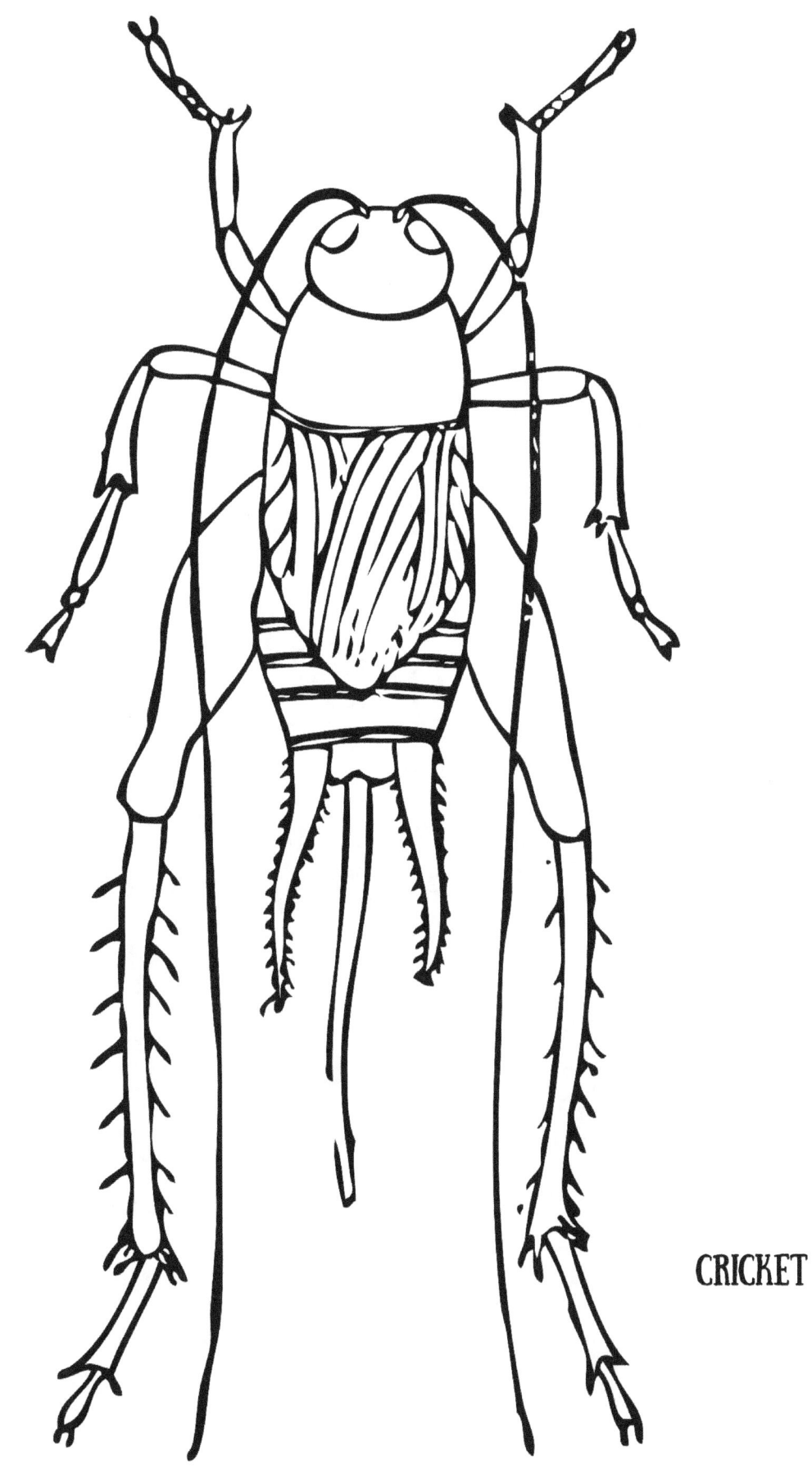

CRICKET

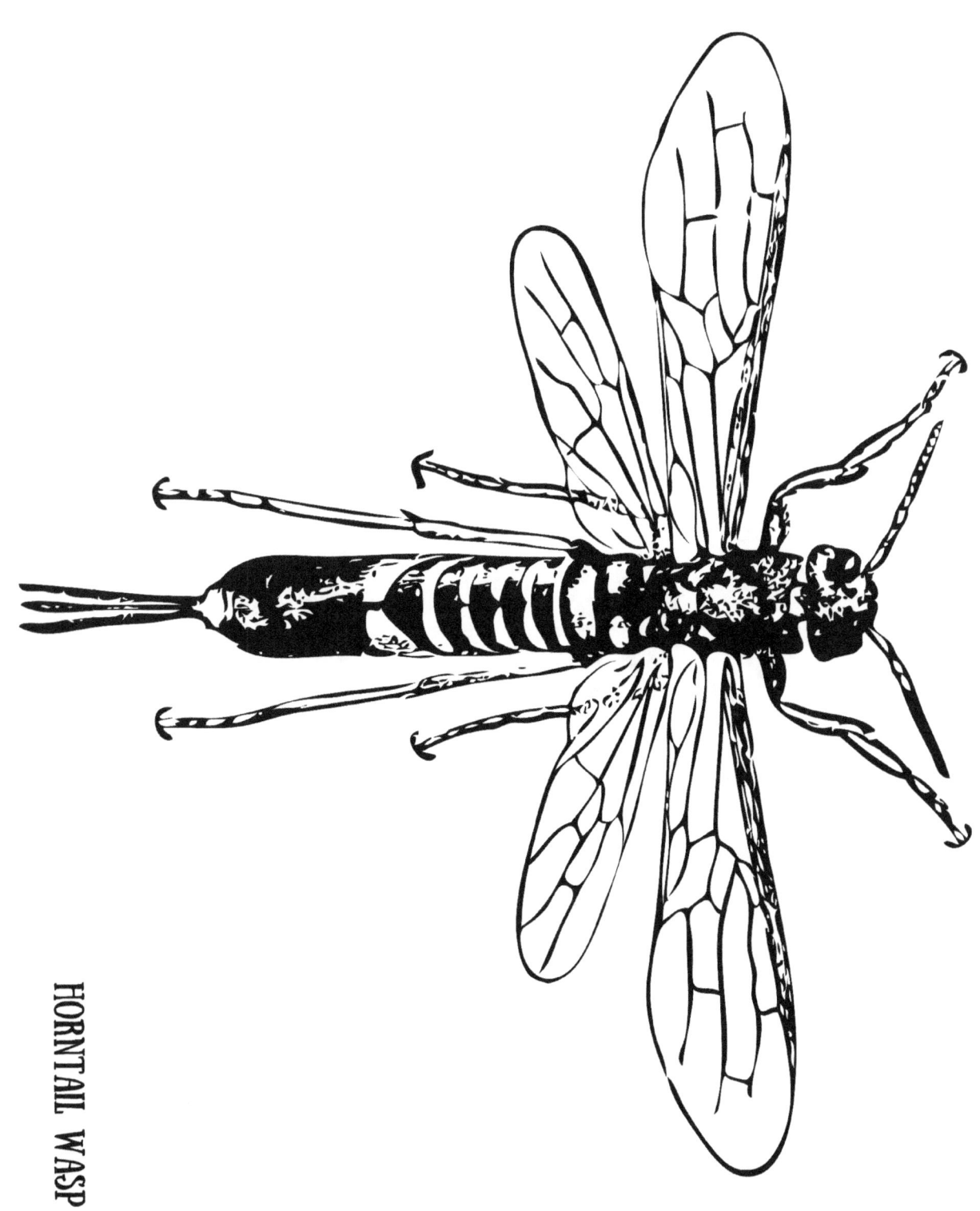

HORNTAIL WASP

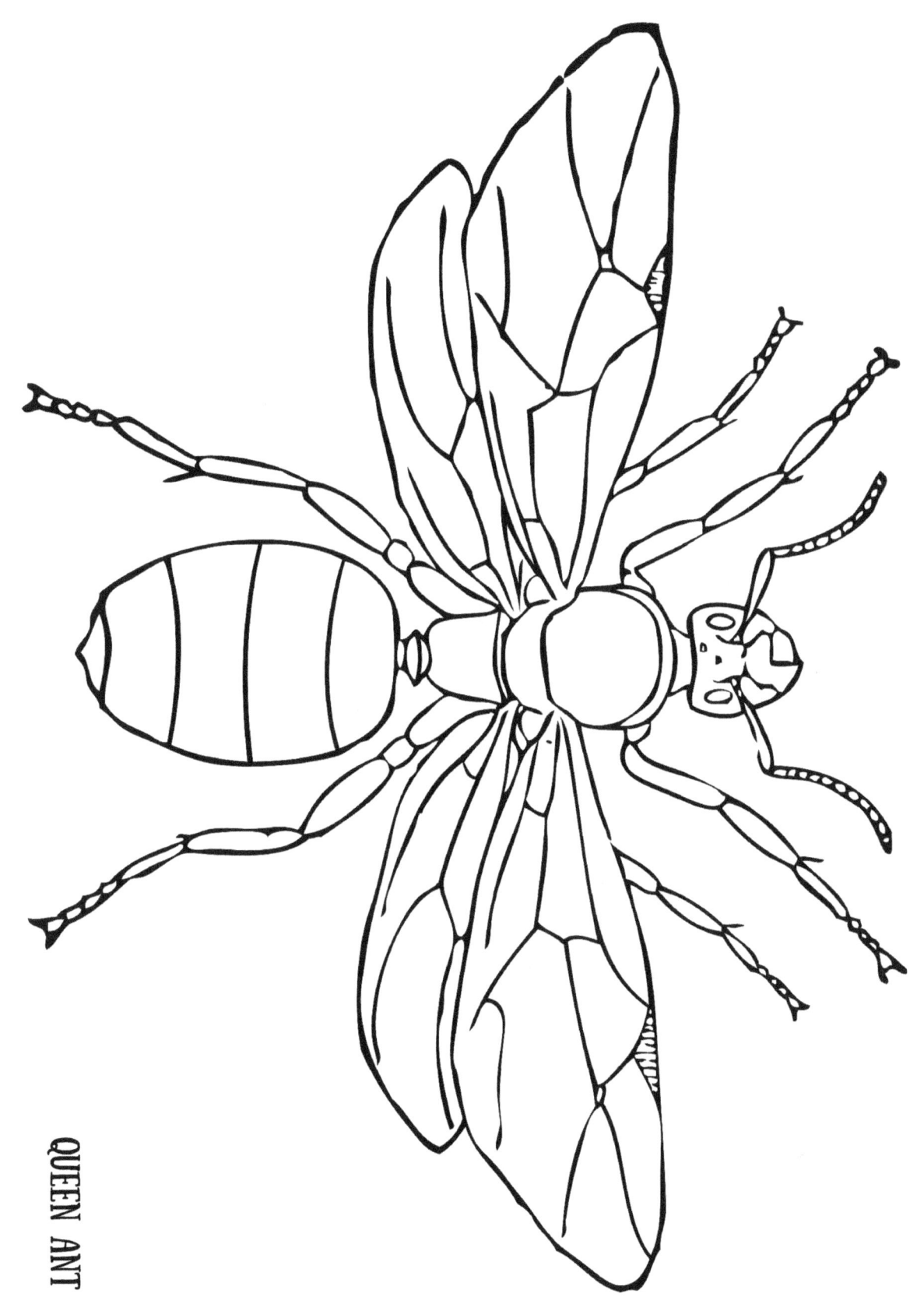

QUEEN ANT

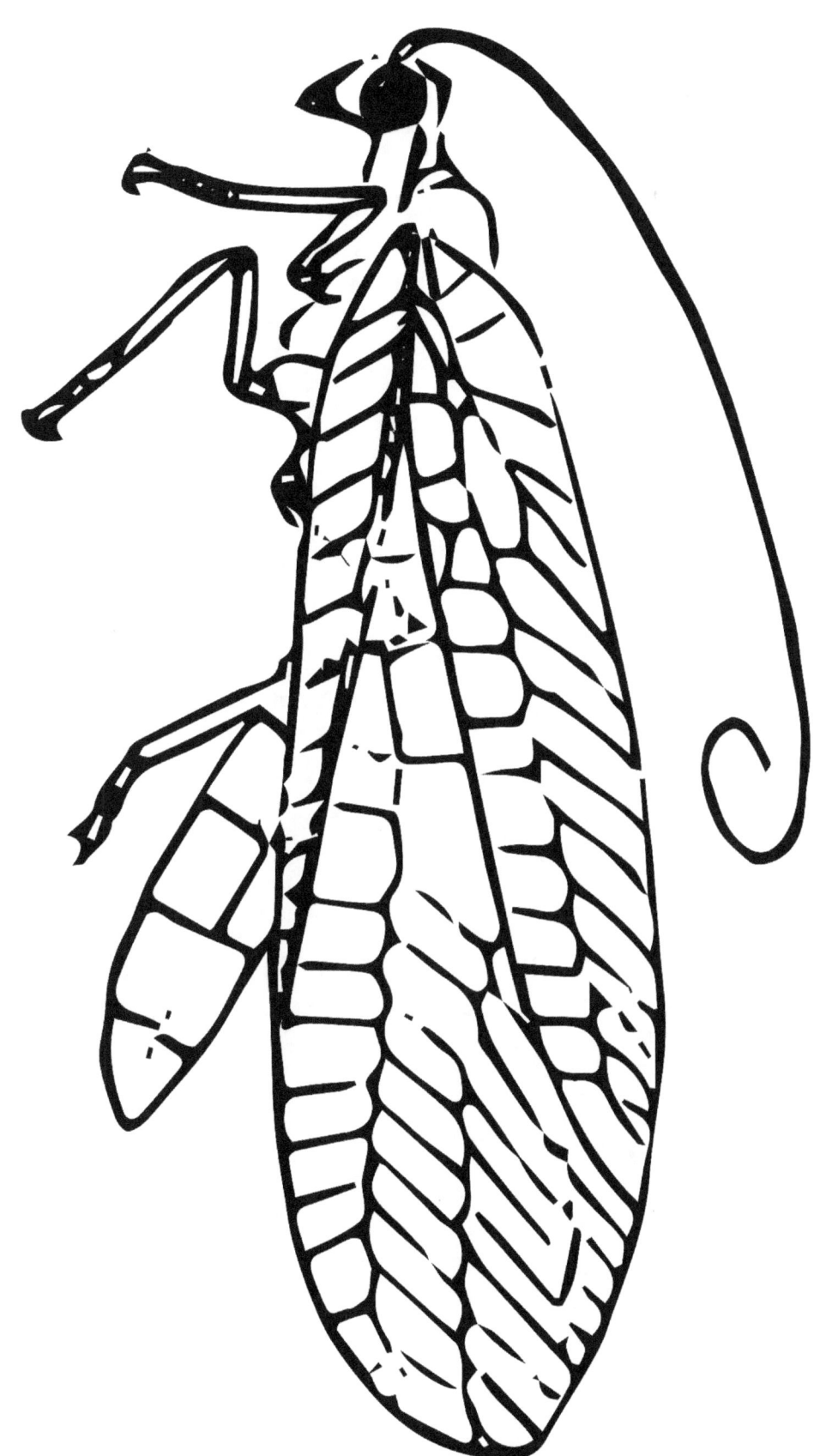

LACEWING

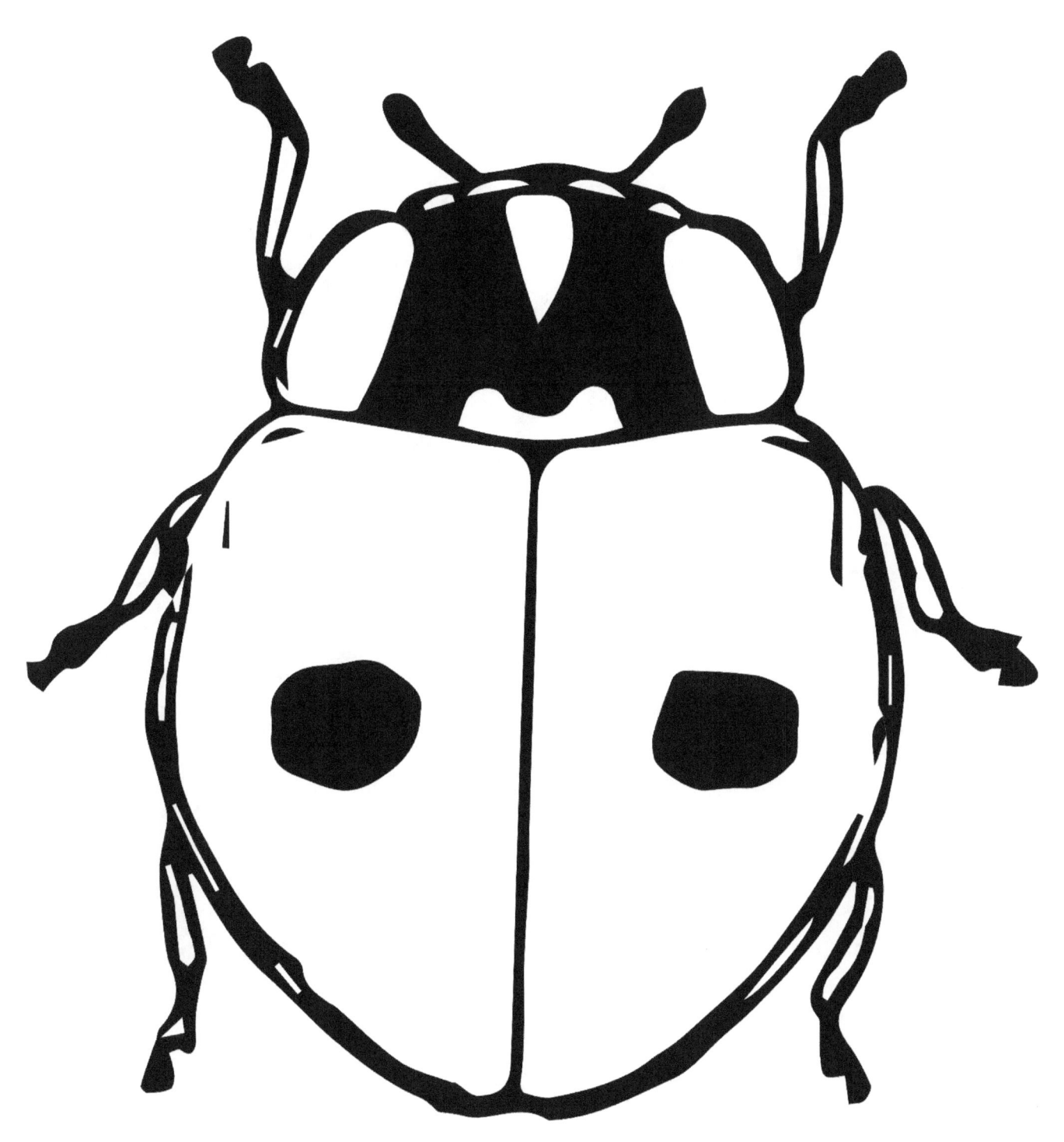

LADY BUG

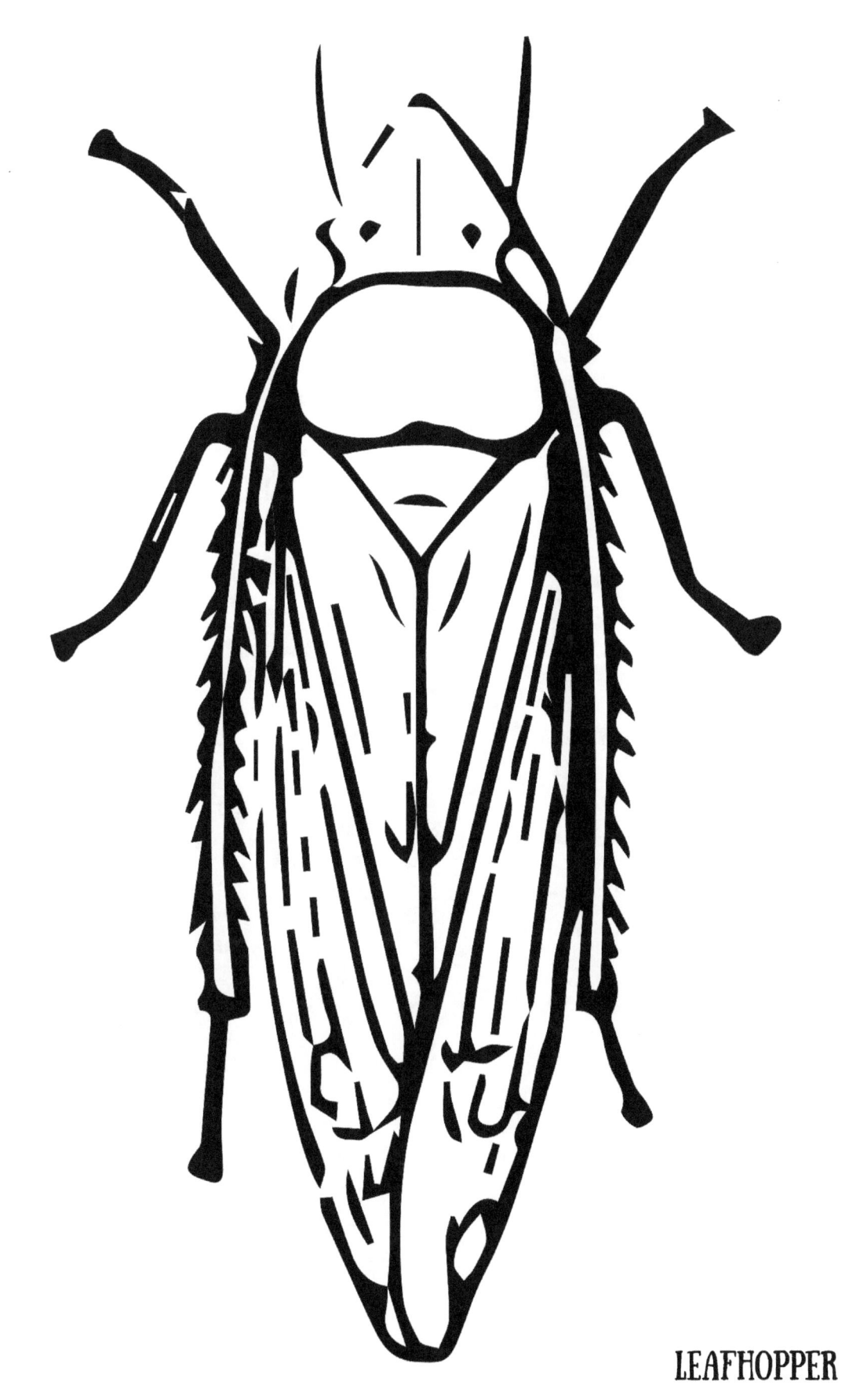

LEAFHOPPER

PRAYING MANTIS

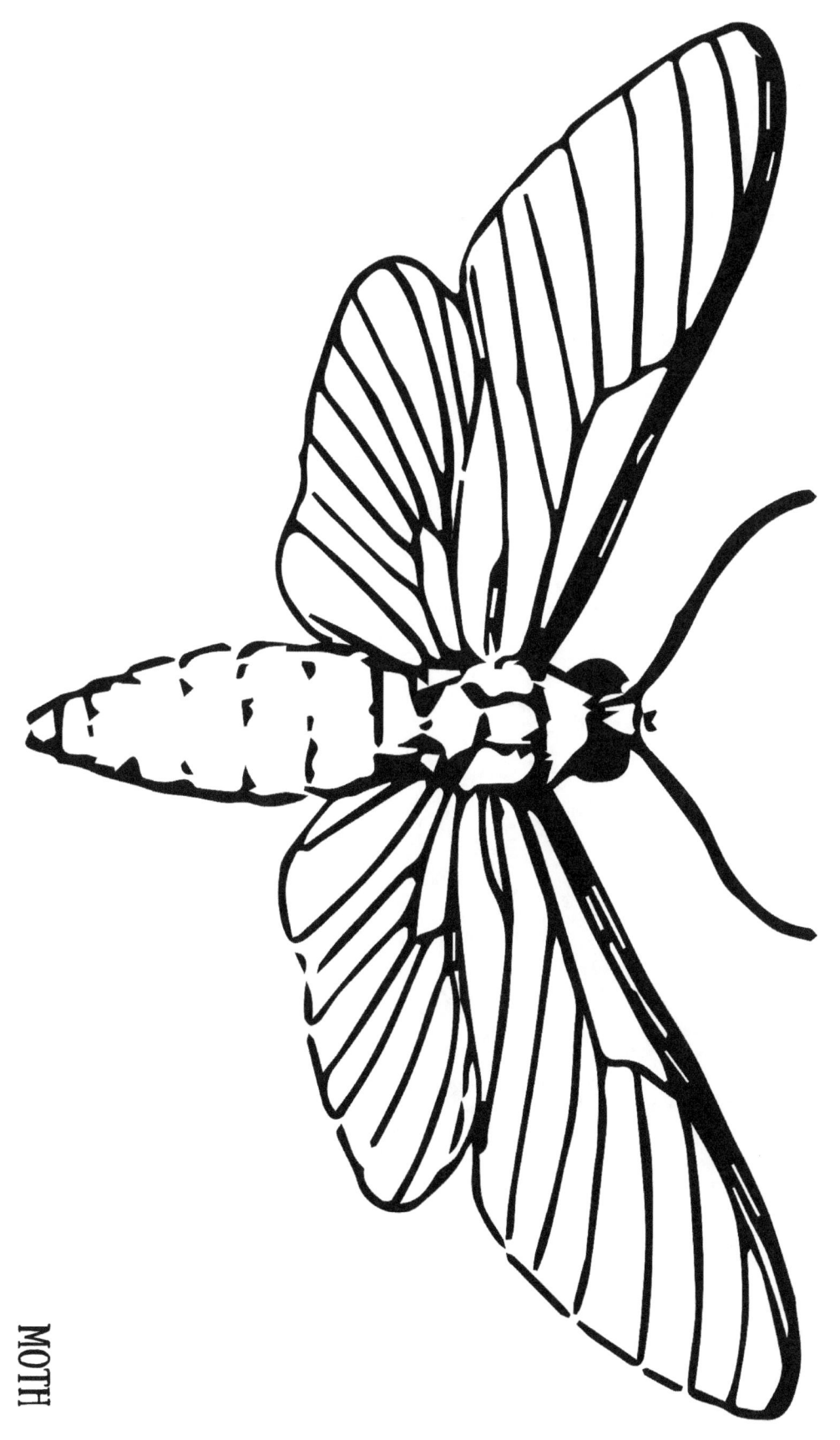

MOTH

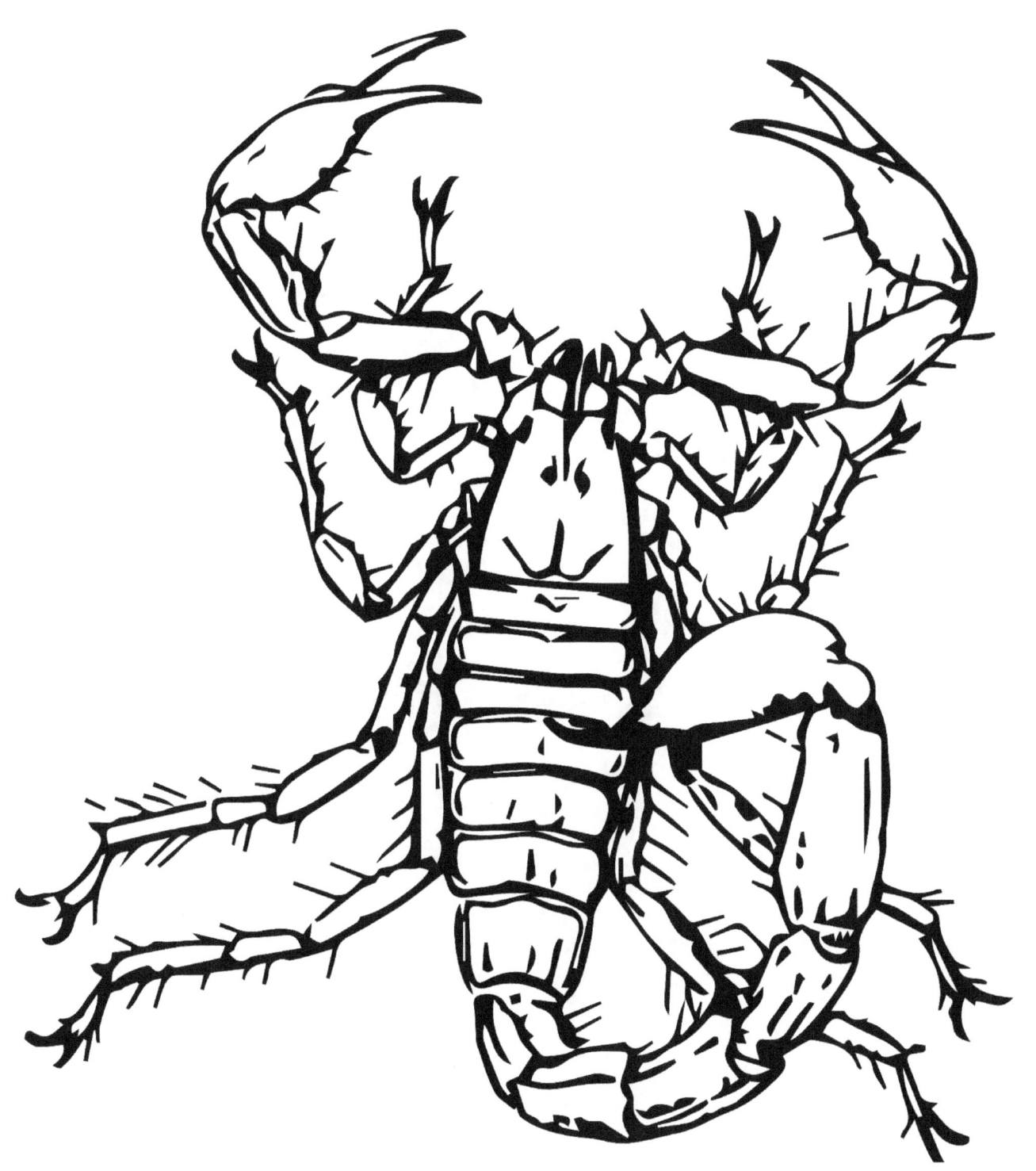

SCORPION

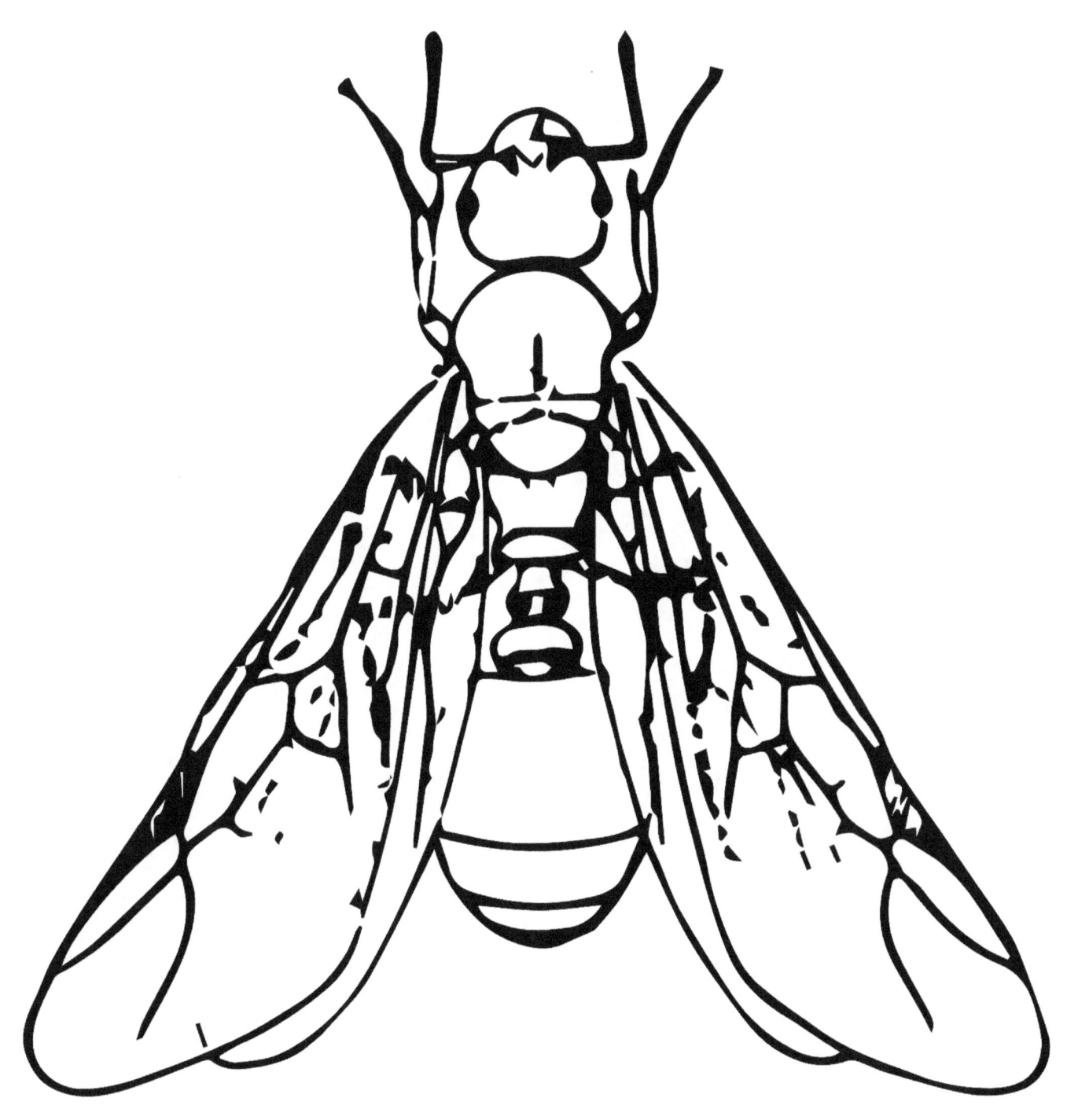

WINGED ANT

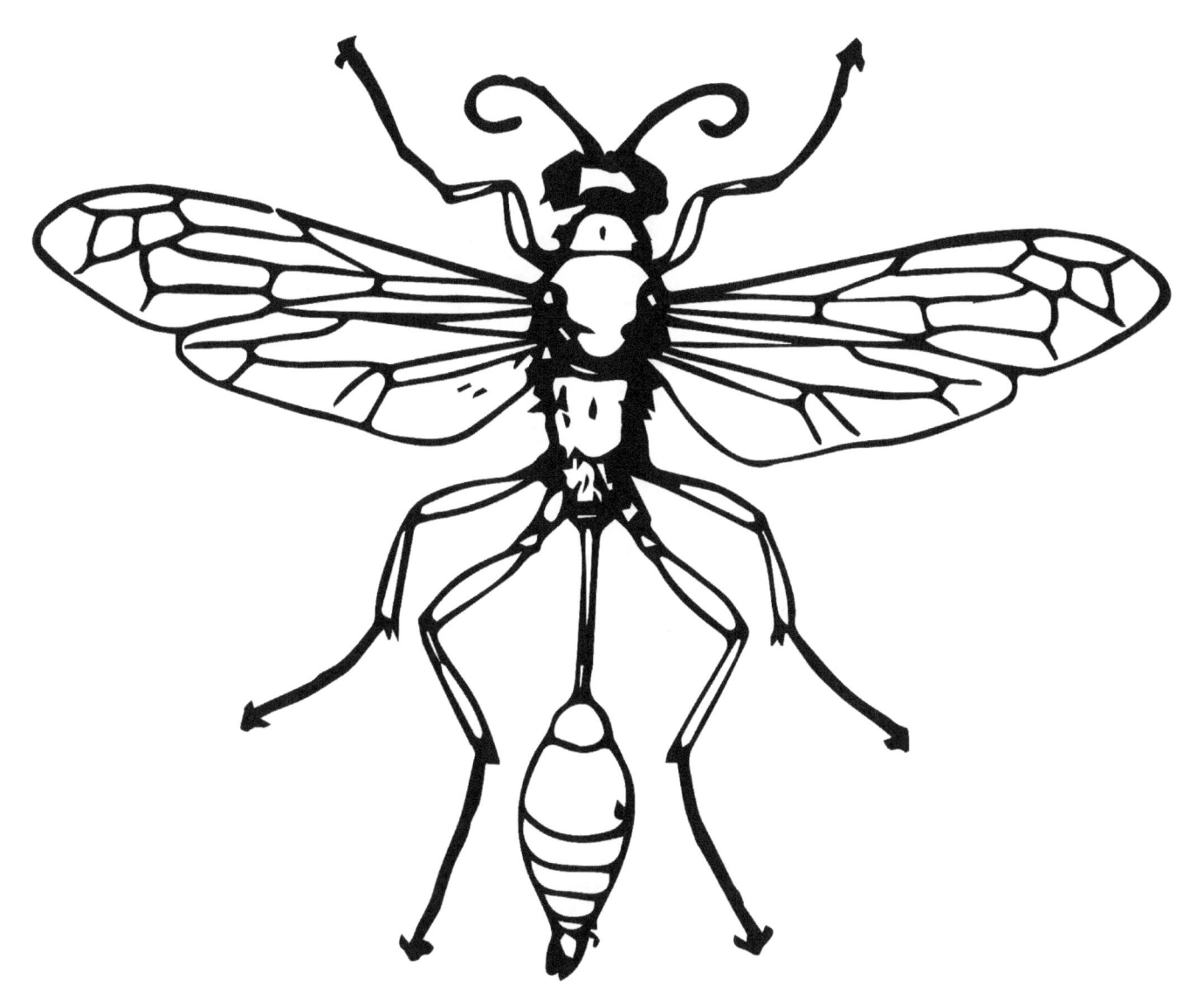

THREAD-WAISTED WASP

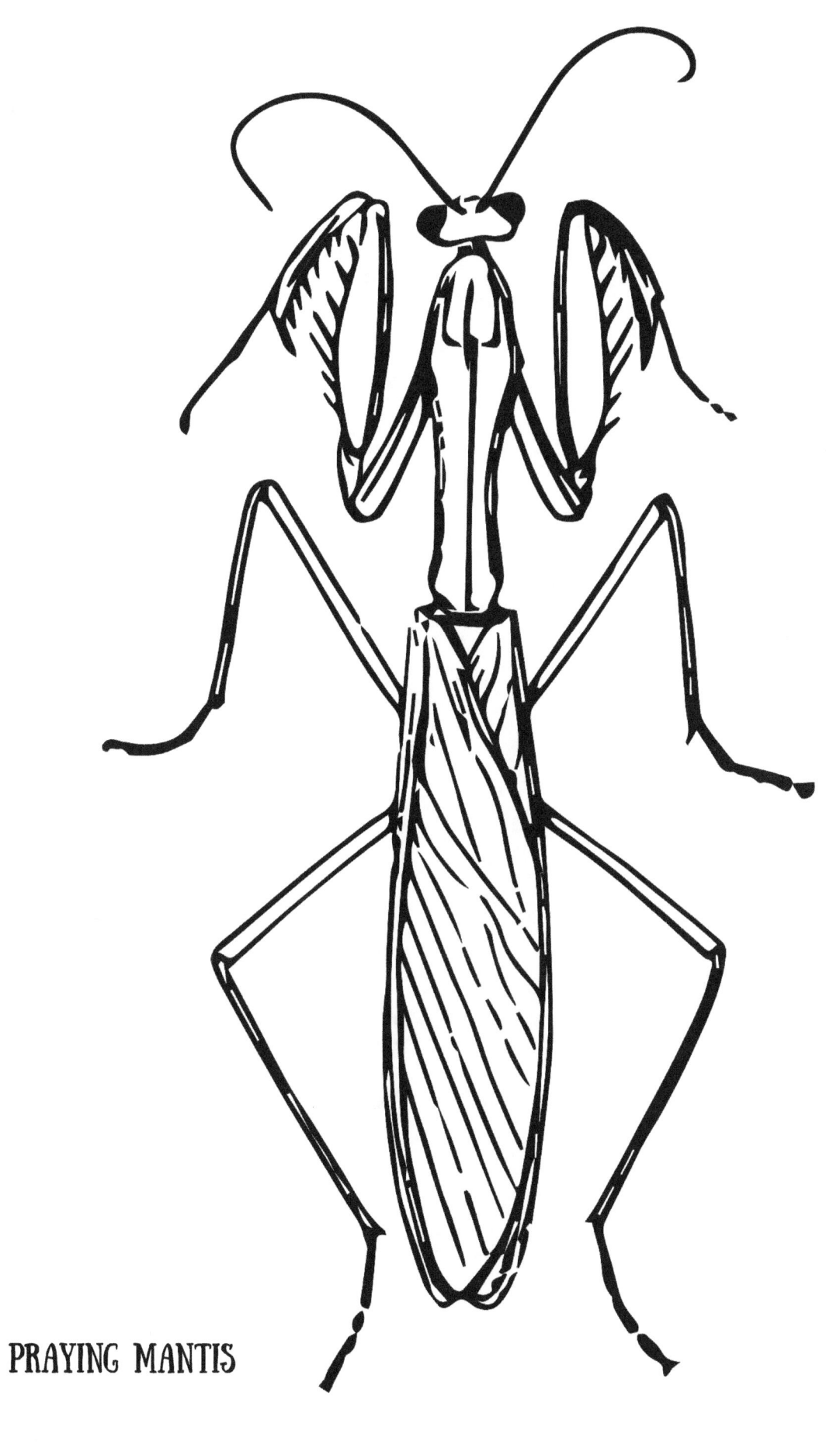

PRAYING MANTIS

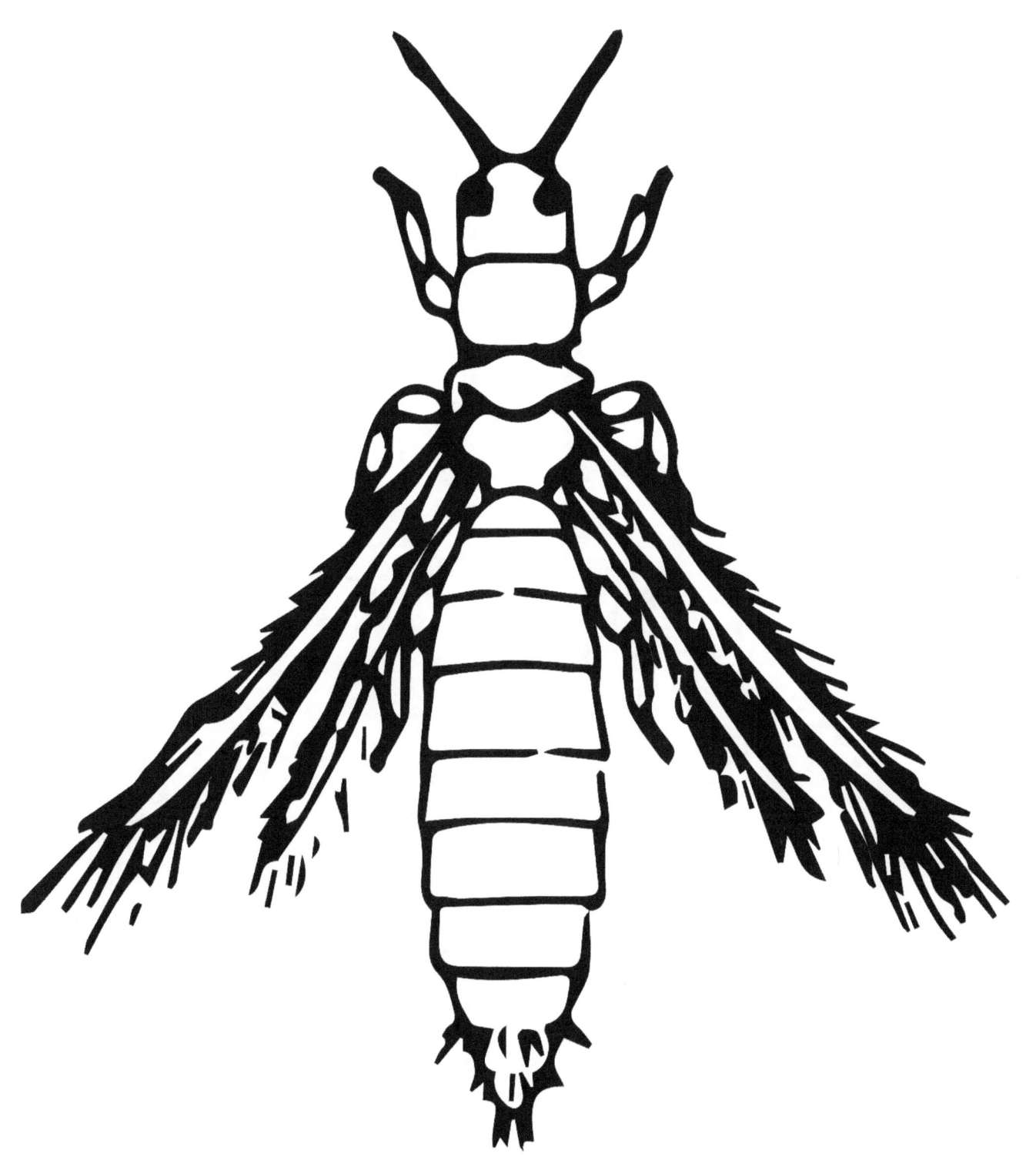

THRIPS

www.ingramcontent.com/pod-product-compliance
Lightning Source LLC
Chambersburg PA
CBHW080548190526
45169CB00007B/2684